SPORTS IN ACTION

Hockey
in Action

Niki Walker & Sarah Dann

🌳 Crabtree Publishing Company

Created by Bobbie Kalman

To Michael Sifuentes and your proud Canadian mom, Suzanne

Editor-in-Chief
Bobbie Kalman

Writing team
Niki Walker
Sarah Dann
John Crossingham

Managing editor
Lynda Hale

Editors
Kate Calder
Heather Levigne

Computer design
Lynda Hale
Niki Walker
Robert MacGregor (cover concept)

Consultant
Paul J. Theriault, Head Coach,
Sault Ste. Marie Greyhounds, OHL

Special thanks to
David Cosgrove, Andrew Corolis, Graham Jenner, Graham Lowe, Dave
Murray, Philip Scott, Carina von Bredow, Anne Kubu, Paul Lewis, and
Ridley College; Dr. George Shunock; Josh Wiwcharyk; Michael Caruso;
Kevin Levigne; Mike Levigne; Blake Malcolm

Photographs and reproductions
Bongarts Photography/SportsChrome: pages 30-31; Marc Crabtree:
front cover, title page, pages 8, 9, 12, 13 (both), 14, 15, 16, 18, 20 (both),
22 (both), 23 (top left & right), 24, 25 (both), 26, 27 (all); Bruce Curtis:
pages 4, 6, 19, 23 (bottom); Brian Drake/SportsChrome: page 28

Illustrations
Trevor Morgan: pucks throughout book, pages 5, 6, 7, 8, 9
Bonna Rouse: back cover, pages 10-11, 15, 16-17, 19, 21

Production coordinator
Hannelore Sotzek

Digital prepress
Embassy Graphics

Printer
Worzalla Publishing Company

Crabtree Publishing Company

PMB 16A
350 Fifth Avenue,
Suite 3308
New York, NY
10118

360 York Road
RR 4
Niagara-on-the-Lake,
Ontario, Canada
L0S 1J0

73 Lime Walk
Headington,
Oxford
OX3 7AD
United Kingdom

Cataloging in Publication Data
Walker, Niki
    Hockey in action

(Sports in action)
Includes index.

ISBN 0-7787-0160-3 (library bound) ISBN 0-7787-0172-7 (pbk.)
This book introduces the techniques, equipment, rules, and safety
requirements of hockey.

1. Hockey—Juvenile literature. 2. Hockey—Training—Juvenile literature.
[1. Hockey.] I. Dann, Sarah, 1970-   . II. Title. III. Series: Kalman, Bobbie.
Sports in action.

GV847.25.W34 2000   j796.962   LC 99-38038
                                                                   CIP

Contents

What is Hockey? ⚬

Hockey is one of the world's fastest team sports. It is the only sport played with a **puck**. The object of a hockey game is to shoot the puck into the opposing team's net and score as many goals as possible. Players from two teams weave and dodge as they skate across the ice. Hockey players need good skating and passing skills in order to keep the puck away from their opponents while they try to score.

Three periods make a game

Most professional hockey games are divided into three 20-minute sections called **periods**. Younger players play ten- or twelve-minute periods. The team that scores the most goals wins the game. Sometimes the score is tied at the end of the third period. In this case, the game goes into a final five-minute period called **overtime**. As soon as one team scores to break the tie, the game is over.

In the beginning...

Most people believe that a sport similar to hockey was played in Europe hundreds of years ago. Some think hockey was born in England as a winter version of field hockey; some say France was its birthplace, and others argue that it was Holland. By the early 1800s, people in North America were playing hockey on outdoor rinks.

In 1875, the first official hockey game was held at McGill University in Montreal, Canada. A group of university students devised a set of rules, which became the basis for the rules used today.

The original six

The **National Hockey League**, or **NHL**, employs today's best professional hockey players. The league formed in Montreal in 1917. The first four teams were the Montreal Wanderers, the Montreal Canadiens, the Toronto Arenas, and the Ottawa Senators.

From 1942 to 1967, the NHL had only six teams—the Boston Bruins, New York Rangers, Chicago Blackhawks, Detroit Cougars (later Red Wings), Toronto Maple Leafs, and Montreal Canadiens. Hockey fans know these teams as the "original six." Since 1967, many new teams have been added. Today there are more than 25 teams.

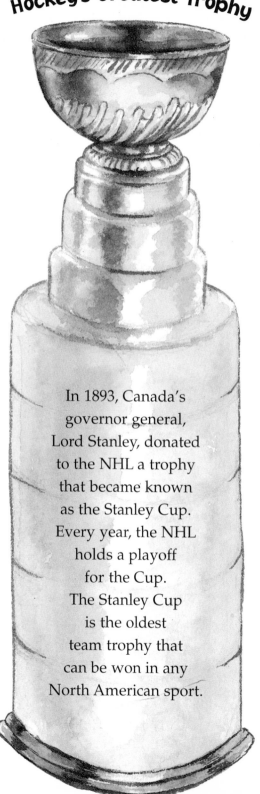

Hockey's Greatest Trophy

In 1893, Canada's governor general, Lord Stanley, donated to the NHL a trophy that became known as the Stanley Cup. Every year, the NHL holds a playoff for the Cup. The Stanley Cup is the oldest team trophy that can be won in any North American sport.

Around the Rink

Hockey games are played on a smooth ice **rink**. Most rinks are in **arenas**, which keep the ice frozen even in warm weather. Hockey rinks are marked with lines and circles that divide the ice into different zones. Each member of a team plays a different **position**, which means he or she has a particular job to do in a certain area of the rink.

Dividing lines

Several lines divide a hockey rink into sections. Two **blue lines** divide the ice into three zones—two **end zones** and a **neutral zone** in the middle. The end with a team's net is its **defensive zone**.

The end with the opposing team's net is the **offensive zone**. The **red line** marks center ice and divides the neutral zone in half.

Switching sides

In a hockey game, each team tries to gain control of the puck in order to score goals. The team with the puck is on **offense**. They try to keep control of the puck and score goals. The team without the puck is on **defense**. The players on defense try to get the puck back and stop the other team from scoring. Players must be able to switch from offense to defense quickly.

Facing off

In hockey, play always starts with a **face-off**. Face-offs take place in one of the five face-off circles. The referee stands at the center of the circle with one player from each team on either side. The other players stand outside the circle. They cannot move until the referee drops the puck and one of the face-off players touches the puck with his or her stick. Face-offs take place at the start of each period and after each pause in play.

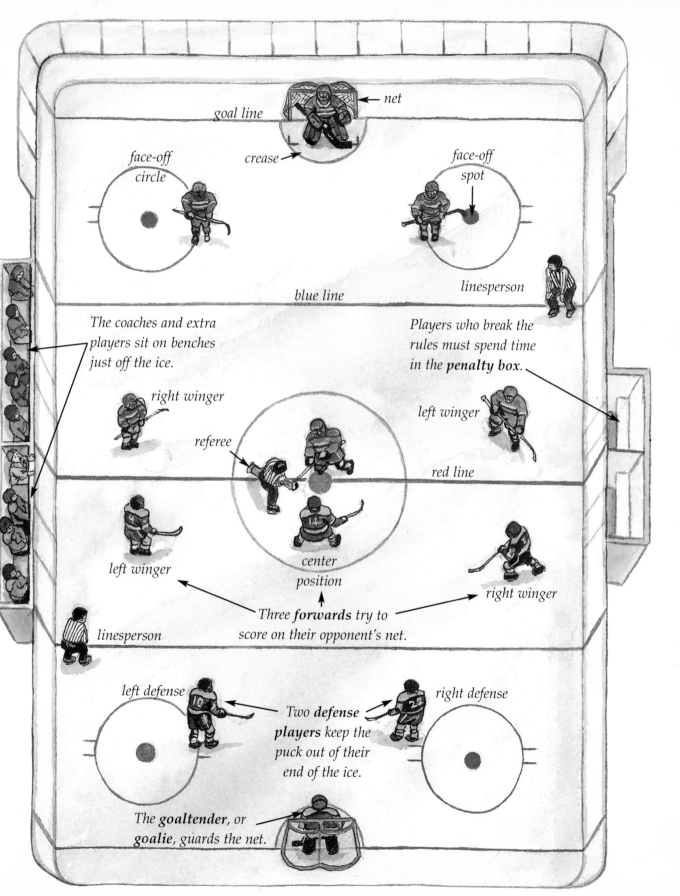

net

goal line

face-off
circle

crease

face-off
spot

linesperson

blue line

The coaches and extra
players sit on benches
just off the ice.

Players who break the
rules must spend time
in the **penalty box**.

right winger

referee

left winger

red line

left winger

center
position

right winger

Three **forwards** try to
score on their opponent's net.

linesperson

left defense

Two **defense
players** keep the
puck out of their
end of the ice.

right defense

The **goaltender**, or
goalie, guards the net.

The Essentials

Most people think of hockey equipment as skates, a stick, a puck, and a net, but hockey players need a lot of safety equipment as well. Players often fall on the ice or get hit by sticks, the puck, or other players, so they need to make sure that their head and body are well protected.

*When playing hockey, always wear a **helmet** and **face guard**. A helmet must fit your head securely so that it does not shift while you're playing.*

shoulder pad

elbow pad

jockstrap

shin guard

Players wear pads under their uniform to protect them from injuries.

sweater

pants

sock

shaft

glove

lie

blade (stick)

heel

blade (skate)

A mask protects the goalie's head and face.

The **blocker** is a glove worn on the hand that holds the stick. It is used to deflect the puck.

The **catcher** is the glove used to grab and hold the puck.

The shaft and blade of a goalie's stick is wide near the bottom to help block the puck.

Goalies wear more padding than other players do. Their arms are padded all the way down to their wrist, and thick pads cover the front of their legs from their skate to their thigh.

Skates are made of leather or lightweight plastic. To keep them in good condition, wipe your skates dry after using them.

Choose a stick with a comfortable length and **lie** for you. The lie is the angle between the shaft and blade. To give you better control of the puck, tape your blade starting at the **heel** and winding toward the tip. Tape the shaft near the top to give you a better grip of the stick.

Gloves protect your hands and keep them warm.

9

Warming Up

Before practicing or playing, it is important to stretch and warm up your muscles. Warming up helps prevent muscle injuries such as strains and pulls. It also gets your body ready to make difficult shots and take falls. These stretches will help you warm up before you try the **drills**, or exercises, in this book.

Do the twist

Place the stick across your shoulders and behind your head. Rest a hand on each end of the stick. Slowly and carefully twist your shoulders to the left and then to the right. Twist only as far as it feels comfortable.

Bend overs

Stand with your feet slightly apart and hold your stick above your head. Slowly bend from the waist. Repeat ten times. Spread your feet farther apart and repeat the stretch ten times.

neck stretch

Tilt your head forward so that your chin points down toward your chest. Slowly roll your head to one shoulder and then to the other. Move your head as far as your shoulder and never more than feels comfortable. Do not roll it all the way back!

Leg lunges

Spread your feet as far apart as you can. Turn your right foot to the side and slowly bend your right knee. Make sure your knee is directly over your toes. Hold the stretch for 15 seconds and then slowly straighten up. Repeat this stretch on the left side.

Trunk circles

Stand with your feet shoulder-width apart and put your hands on your hips. Swing your hips in a circle, keeping your feet flat and your shoulders as still as possible.

Arm circles

Slowly rotate your arms forward in large circles. Keep making smaller circles until your arms are straight out to the side and moving in tiny circles. Now reverse the direction, starting with small circles and ending with giant ones.

High-stick kicks

With your arms outstretched, hold your stick in front of you. Keep your knees slightly bent and lightly hit the stick with your knee. Repeat ten times with each leg.

On the Ice ●

Skating is the first and most important skill hockey players learn. Being able to skate fast, change directions quickly, and stop almost instantly are skills involved in every play.

Take it easy

Skating is a skill that may take you a while to learn. When skating for the first time, take it easy. Leave your stick on the bench and hold out your arms for balance. Make your strides slowly and carefully.

Pushing off

To skate, bend your knee and push one blade into the ice behind you. You will glide forward across the ice on your other skate. Now switch and thrust with the other leg. As you skate, shift your weight from one side to the other. With practice, your skating skills will improve and help you become a better hockey player.

Keeping your body in the proper stance will help you keep your balance. Keep your chin up, knees bent, and back straight.

Crossovers

Crossovers help players skate in fast curves so they can dodge around their opponents. To curve left, lift your right foot, cross it over your left leg, and place it on the ice. Then step forward with your left foot. Keep crossing your right leg over your left foot and stepping forward with your left foot. To gain speed, bend your knees and push off with each leg as you lift it off the ice. Practice doing crossovers in the other direction by crossing your left leg over your right foot.

Whoa!

Skating over ice at high speeds requires the ability to stop and change directions quickly. The **hockey stop** is the fastest way to put on the brakes. To perform a hockey stop, turn your whole body sideways and dig your blades into the ice. Beginners learn to stop using the **snowplow**. To do a snowplow, bend your knees and turn the front of your skates toward one another. You will come to a gradual stop.

Stickhandling

Imagine you are skating down the ice as fast as you can toward your opponents' net. You have the puck, and you know you can score the next goal. The only problem is that there are three opponents between you and the net, and they will try as hard as they can to take the puck away from you. This situation calls for some super **stickhandling** skills!

Moving with the puck

Stickhandling the puck as you skate helps you keep it away from your opponents. To stickhandle, move the puck quickly from side to side or front to back as you skate. This action is also known as **carrying the puck**. When you move the puck around quickly, it is difficult for your opponents to steal the puck from you. Stickhandling also lets you change direction quickly while keeping control of the puck.

*With great stickhandling skills, you'll be able to **rag the puck**. Ragging the puck is keeping it away from your opponents without trying to set up a goal. Players often rag the puck to waste time when it is near the end of the game and their team is in the lead.*

Keep it close

The key to stickhandling is learning how hard you can tap the puck without letting it get too far away from you. Stand still and carry the puck from side to side and front to back. Try tapping the puck back and forth as many times as you can without losing control of it.

Once you are comfortable stickhandling while standing still, try moving forward. Set up an obstacle course with pylons to skate around as you stickhandle. You can also use a friend as a moving "obstacle." Have your friend try to take the puck away from you. Practice carrying the puck without looking down at it. Always keep your head up during a game so you can see where you are going.

If you don't have the option of practicing on ice, use a ball or street-hockey puck to practice on pavement or at the gym. Keeping the puck close to your stick makes it easier to control.

Faking out your opponent

The **deke** is a popular hockey trick. It fools an opponent into thinking you're moving in one direction when you're actually going to skate in another. In this picture, the player in black began to move to her left. As her opponent moved over to block her, she quickly moved to her right and around her opponent. Practice deking with a friend. Set up start and finish lines with pylons. Try to deke past your friend and to the finish line without letting him or her touch you.

Shoot it!

Stickhandling and deking are important skills, but the time will come when you have to shoot the puck! You need to be able to shoot accurately in order to pass it to a teammate or score a goal. There are different ways to shoot the puck. Each one has different uses and will help you get the puck exactly where you want it to go.

power hand

*The hand that is farther along your stick is your **power hand**. You will use it to guide and move your stick.*

Make it comfortable

Are you a right-handed or left-handed player? Which way does it feel more comfortable to hold your stick—to the left or right of your body? Use the side that is most comfortable for you.

Sliding the puck

The slide shot is hockey's basic shot. You can use it to make a pass or take a shot on the net. Push the puck across the surface of the ice. After sliding the puck, continue swinging your stick up off the ice. This move is called the **follow-through**.

*To make a **forehand shot**, shown left, the palm of the power hand should face the target. To make a **backhand shot**, shown right, the back of the power hand should face the target.*

Wrist shot

A wrist shot is a fast, accurate shot. When you make this shot, your stick should always be touching the puck—you shouldn't hear the sound of your stick hitting the puck. As you shoot, flick your wrists so that the fingers of your power hand point upward. The flicking action brings your blade up and under the puck to lift it off the ice. Remember to follow through on your shot.

Flicking your wrists

You will use this wrist action to lift the puck off the ice to make passes and take shots at the net.

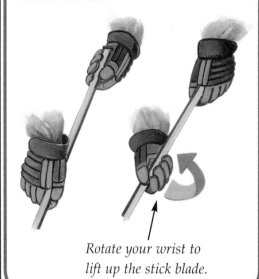

Rotate your wrist to lift up the stick blade.

Snap shot

A snap shot is similar to a wrist shot, but you flick your wrists just before you hit the puck. Do not follow through with your stick. Unlike a wrist shot, when you make a snap shot you will hear the sound of your stick hitting the puck.

Slap shot

Slap shots have a large windup and follow-through. When shooting a slap shot, keep your power arm straight and rotate your shoulders with the shot.

17

Passing •

Passing is an important skill to master. Your teammates won't be happy if you always keep the puck to yourself. It's often better to pass the puck to one of your teammates than to risk letting an opponent steal it. Passing also lets you get the puck quickly to a teammate who is in position to score. Passing to a player who then scores a goal is called an **assist**.

The key to passing is aiming and shooting the puck with the right amount of force. The only way to learn these skills is to practice them over and over.

Slide on over!

Although a pass should be made quickly, it should also be easy for your teammate to receive. The slide shot (see page 16) is the best shot to use for passing. The puck travels on the ice, so it is easy to stop.

On the receiving end

Keep your blade on the ice when you're waiting for a pass. As the puck reaches your stick blade, keep your arms relaxed and let the stick move back slightly with the puck. Moving your stick back lets you receive and control the puck more easily.

Lifting the puck

Sometimes you'll find it impossible to get the puck to a teammate using a slide pass. Use a wrist shot to lift the puck off the ice and over an obstacle such as an opponent's stick. Practice lifting the puck by placing a small object, such as a stick or glove, between you and your friend. Lift the puck to one another over the obstacle, using both forehand and backhand shots.

Try to shoot the puck accurately so that your partner does not have to move his or her feet to receive it.

Leading the puck

The pass in this picture is too far behind Number 18. She must slow down and turn around in order to receive the pass. Players must **lead the puck** when passing to a teammate who is skating. To lead the puck, send it ahead of where your teammate is at the moment you pass so that the puck and the player will end up in the same spot at the same time.

Take Your Best Shot

The goaltender has to be ready to take shots from many different angles. Players aim for one of the holes the goalie is not covering. This goalie is in a position to defend two of the holes, but three holes are still open. Could you get the puck past him?

Imagine that your team is losing a game by one point, there are only a few seconds left on the clock, and you have the puck. As you get ready to shoot, you picture the puck whizzing into the net and the crowd cheering loudly. Scoring a goal in a real game, however, is more difficult than you might imagine. You first have to get the puck past your opponents!

The five holes

To become a master scorer, you must practice every chance you get. Hockey players and coaches have figured out the five areas where it is easiest to get the puck past the goalie. These spots are called **holes**.

Target practice

If you're practicing alone, set up targets at which to aim. Use the photo on page 20 as a model and draw five spots on a wall with chalk or cut five holes out of a large piece of cardboard. Stand in front of your targets and take shots at each of the five spots. Which target do you find easiest to hit? Which one is hardest? Set goals for yourself. Aim at one target until you can hit it three times in a row before you aim for a different one. When you can hit all the targets, make the drill more difficult. You can change the spot you are shooting from, use different types of shots, or move toward the target as you shoot.

One on one

With a friend, practice taking shots while moving. The puck handler starts moving toward the net, and the defender tries to take away the puck before the handler can shoot. If the handler scores, he or she gets to start again from another spot. If he or she misses, the other player becomes the puck handler. Each goal scored is one point.

Goaltending

Goalies need to be fast and agile. They wait for other players to send the small, hard puck whizzing toward their head and body. Most people would duck or jump out of the way, but goalies do whatever it takes to put themselves between the puck and the net.

Stop that puck!

Stopping a puck from going into the net is called **making a save**. There are many ways goalies can make a save. They can catch the puck and hold it or **freeze** the puck on the ice by covering it with their glove or body. When they can't stop the puck, goalies try to **deflect it**, or knock it away, with their stick, blocker, skates, or pads.

*(above) This goalie is making a **deck save**. He throws his body across the front of the net, sliding on his side with his stick out as far as possible. Deck saves block most of the lower part of the net.*

*(left) Goalies wait for a shot in the **ready stance**— leaning forward, chin up, and knees together and bent. They hold their stick in front, ready to stop a shot.*

This goalie is demonstrating the **V-save**. In this position, he uses his legs to block a puck sliding toward the net.

This goalie is making a **blocker save**. He deflects the puck with his blocker. When making a **glove save**, the goalie uses his catcher to grab the puck from the air.

Behind a screen

Can you spot the goalie in the picture on the right? When a number of players are in front of the net, it is difficult for the goalie to see the puck. This situation is called **screening**. To prevent a goal, the goalie needs to bend closer to the ice because it is easier to see past the players' legs and skates than their bulky, padded upper body.

Checking

Each team wants to have control of the puck in order to score goals. Getting control of the puck takes a lot of determination! Players can use their stick or their body to **check**, or steal the puck from another player. Most leagues do not allow players under thirteen years of age to **body check** opponents, so this book will show you only how to **stick check**.

Handle with care

Older, experienced players often use a body check to get control of the puck. They bump their opponent with their body, causing the player to lose control of the puck. Body checking must be done correctly, however, or someone could get hurt. The purpose of a body check is to unbalance your opponents, not to knock them out!

Lift check

The player in yellow has surprised his opponent with a **lift check**. To perform a lift check, skate up alongside the puck handler and slip your stick shaft under his or her stick. Now quickly lift your stick, raising your opponent's stick long enough for you to scoop the puck and skate away.

Poke check

The **poke check** is useful when your opponent is skating toward you. Here, the player in the black sweater is holding her stick with just one hand. When the yellow player is within reach, she quickly pokes her stick forward and knocks the puck away from him.

forward

defender

Sweep check

The player in the black sweater is using a **sweep check** to knock her opponent's stick away from the puck. A sweep check is often done while holding the stick with one hand. To perform a sweep check, skate backwards and swing your stick against your opponent's so he or she loses control of the puck.

defender

forward

25

Penalties and Power Plays

Hockey has rules that help keep the game fair and safe. Some rules forbid certain actions. Players who break these rules receive penalties and must sit in the penalty box. Depending on the penalty and the referee's judgment, they could get a **minor** or **major** penalty. A minor penalty is two minutes in the box, and a major penalty is five minutes.

All the wrong moves

Most penalties happen when a player tries to check an opponent unfairly. For example, **spearing** occurs when a player uses his or her stick to jab an opponent's body. If you make any of the wrong moves shown on these two pages, you'll find yourself sitting in the penalty box! Remember that fighting is not allowed and it can get you thrown out of the game.

Power up!

When one team gets a penalty, it is easier for the other team to score. While you're sitting in the penalty box, your team is **short-handed**, or has fewer players on the ice. When one team has more players on the ice than the other team, the situation is known as a **power play**. It is easier for a team on a power play to score a goal.

*Hitting a player from behind can cause an injury. You can get kicked out of the game for this type of checking. If you push a player a short distance into the boards, the referee may call **boarding**, which is a minor penalty. Pushing a player a greater distance with more force is called **checking from behind**, which is a more serious penalty.*

Hooking

Hooking is using your stick to hold an opponent's stick, arms, or body. It is a minor penalty.

High-sticking

High-sticking, or hitting a player above the shoulders with your stick, is a minor or major penalty, depending on the referee's judgment.

Slashing

Slashing, or swinging your stick at another player's body, is not only against the rules, it is dangerous. You can get a major penalty for slashing.

Tripping

Tripping another player with your stick or skate, even if it is an accident, will also result in a minor penalty. Tripping an opponent on a **breakaway** from behind can result in a **penalty shot**. In a penalty shot, the player who is tripped gets a free shot on the net.

Enforcing the Rules

Without the referee, two linespersons, goal judges, and an official scorer, a hockey game would be chaotic! The referee is the leader of all officials and has the final say when rules are broken. Players, coaches, and fans may disagree with a call made by a referee, but his or her decision is final.

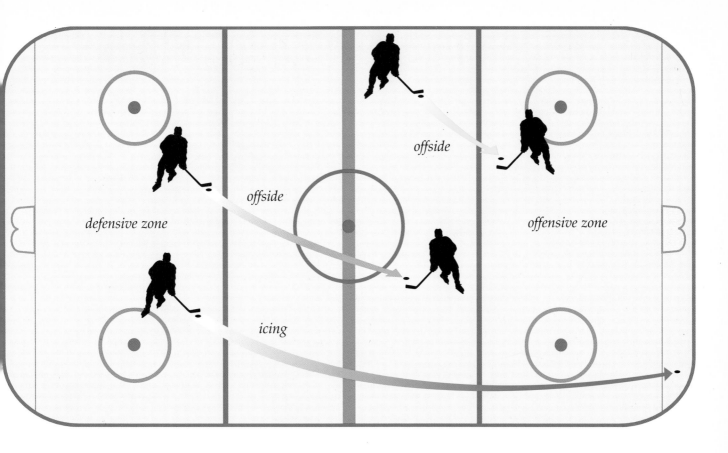

offside

offside

defensive zone

offensive zone

icing

Stopping play

The referee blows the whistle and stops play many times during a hockey game. He or she stops play when the puck is shot out of the rink, a player other than the goalie covers up the puck, a player is caught **offside**, **icing** occurs, or to give penalties.

Offside? What's that?

The offside rule prevents players from waiting by their opponent's net for an easy goal. A player is offside when he or she moves across the other team's blue line before the puck does. The referee

also calls an **offside pass** if a player passes the puck to a teammate across both the blue line and the center line. This type of pass is also called a **two-line pass**. After the referee blows the whistle, play stops and the players must face off in the neutral zone.

Icing on the rink

Icing occurs when a player hits the puck from his or her half of the rink, and it crosses the opponent's goal line without another player touching it. Icing is not called against a team that is playing short-handed.

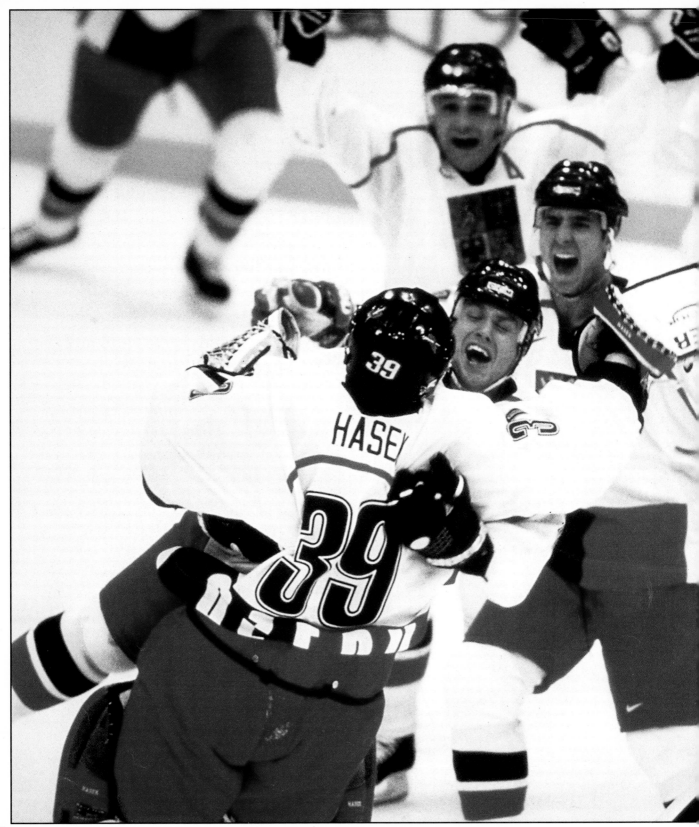

Play Like a Pro

Many young athletes dream of playing professional hockey someday. Of the thousands of young people who play hockey, few will ever make the NHL. Everyone else can still have fun playing, though. Joining a hockey team and playing in a league can teach you many valuable skills that you'll use off the ice. Besides, you don't have to be a pro to impress people— just learn the facts on this page and you can amaze your friends and teammates with your knowledge of hockey!

The longest overtime game on record happened during the Stanley Cup playoffs in 1936. After almost two hours of overtime, the Montreal Maroons finally lost to the Detroit Red Wings.

Hockey was the first sport in which players wore numbers on the back of their sweater.

More than one player on a team can be in the penalty box at the same time, but a team must always have at least three players on the ice.

The name "hockey" may have come from the French word *hoquet*, which means "bent stick."

In the NHL, pucks are frozen before the game so they will slide better and bounce less.

Most players dream of scoring a **hat trick**, or three goals in a single game. A pure hat trick happens when the same player scores three goals in a row.

Hockey Words

breakaway A situation in which a player has an opportunity to score without interference from anyone but the goalie

check To steal the puck by knocking it away from your opponent with your body or stick

crease The area directly in front of the net in which only the goalie is permitted to stand

defense (1) The players on a team who play between the goalie and the forwards; (2) Describing the team that does not have the puck

deke To pretend to move in one direction but then move in another

forward One of three positions on a team—center, left wing, or right wing

goaltender The person who stands in front of the net and tries to stop goals from being scored

linesperson An official who assists the referee

offense (1) The players who are a team's forwards; (2) Describing the team with the puck

offside When a player moves over the blue line ahead of the puck

penalty A punishment given to a player who breaks a rule

power play A situation in which one team has more players on the ice because the opposing team has one or more players in the penalty box

puck A hard rubber disk

screening A situation in which players stand in front of the goalie, blocking his or her view of the puck

stickhandle To move the puck quickly back and forth or from side to side while skating

Index

1 2 3 4 5 6 7 8 9 0   Printed in the U.S.A.   8 7 6 5 4 3 2 1 0 9